The
Saints
of the
California
Landscape

Padre Junípero Serra

The
Saints
of the
California
Landscape

by
Raymund F. Wood

———————— ◯ ————————

Illustrated
by
Anthony Quartuccio

Prosperity Press   Eagle Rock, CA   1987

Library of Congress Cataloging-in-Publication Data

Wood, Raymund F.
    The saints of the California landscape.

    Bibliography: p. viii
1. Names, Geographical--California. 2. Christian saints--
Biography. 3. California--History, Local. I. Title.
F859.W66 1987   917.94'003'21   86-30458
ISBN 0-87062-176-9

distributed by: R. F. Wood
               18052 Rosita St.
               Encino, CA 91316

PREFACE

Visitors to California, as well as residents, are often intrigued by the large number of places in California named for saints, angels, and other aspects of religion, such as Point Concepcion, or the cities of San Francisco, Los Angeles, and Sacramento, the state capital.

This gives rise to two often-asked questions: 1) what is a saint? and 2) why are there so many places in California named for them?

1) What is a saint?

A saint is a person who once lived a life on this earth (excluding for the moment the three named archangels), and while on this earth did either one of two things (or sometimes did both) -- he or she lived a life of heroic virtue, or he or she was martyred. In the latter case this means that the person was executed, often after torture, primarily or exclusively because of being a Christian.

During the first three centuries, from about the reign of the emperor Nero (A.D. 54-68) until the Edict of Milan in 313, many hundreds, if not thousands, of Christians were condemned to death. During these three centuries there were ten identifiable periods of intense persecution, each one lasting only a short period of time. These usually occured when some energetic emperor decided to enforce the general laws which forbade the worship of any god other than the Roman ones, whom the Christians regarded as false gods. But the ten periods of persecution were quite harsh, and many families, from every walk of life, were denounced, brought before magistrates, and finally executed, often in very cruel ways.

All such persons were believed by the surviving faithful to have had their sins washed away by the shedding of their blood, and to be in heaven. Such a person (in Latin a "sanctus," from a word meaning "to set apart by a religious act"), was thought to be different from ordinary persons; in other words, a saint. At first the only saints were the martyrs, and all martyrs were held to be saints.

But when the persecutions ended, and men and women of holy life came to die of natural causes, the Church needed to recognize their holiness in some way. Often it was by regional popular acclaim. The townspeople knew that a certain person had led a holy life. So, after his or her death they prayed and asked for favors. Frequently they received these divine favors, which they attributed to the holy person's intercession. Very many saints were thus incorporated into the Church's Calendar of Saints, and many miracles were worked by their intercession.

As the centuries went by there arose a need to distinguish ordinary holiness from what came to be termed "heroic virtue." The central authority of the Church, the Papacy, felt that it was time to establish rules, and to set up a "canon" or register of those who were truly saints. The earliest such action took place in 993, but it was not until 1170 that the Pope declared officially that no new saints were to be acclaimed without due investigation by, and permission of, the Papacy. Finally, by decrees of Pope Urban VIII in 1625 and in 1634, the process of "canonization" was set up.

This process involves three major steps. First a declaration that the person is "Venerable," and may be the object of private devotion. Next, after considerable scrutiny of the person's life, and writings if any, and the verification of at least one miracle, the person is beatified, that is to say, declared to be "Blessed." Finally, the full step of "canonization," in which the Pope decrees the fullness of public honors; the name is added to the Canon of the Saints; and the faithful are entitled to refer to that person as "Saint ...". This last step can only occur after at least one additional miracle can be verified as having been performed through the Blessed's intercession with God, since the date of the Decree of Beatification.

It is the firm belief of Catholics that such persons are indeed in heaven; that by the power of God they can receive prayers addressed to them; and that upon occasion a miraculous healing, such as those at Lourdes, may be performed by the hand of God through the Saint's intercession.

2) Why are there so many saints' names in California?

The answer is, first, that the earliest explorers, in 1542, 1602, 1769, and later, were Spanish Catholics, and it was common custom in their world to denote landmarks, rivers, valleys, mountains, native villages and so on, by the name of the saint whose feast was celebrated on or near the day such landmarks were visited or first seen. Both priests and soldiers participated in the naming of these landmarks, but the soldiers were less likely to be familiar with the calendar of saints' days, and they often named places after some incident of the day, the discovery of a wild animal, the loss of a weapon, or the location of a good spring of water. But more usually it was the priest-diarist who recorded the name and date of the saint whose festival it was that day, and most of these names have survived.

Second, many of the the cities of today's California arose from the twenty-one Franciscan missions established for the conversion of the natives. Each mission had a patron saint (including the three archangels, who were given the honorary title of "Saint").

Third, other places in California arose from land grants, which in turn were often named for a saint, or had a saint's name in their title.

Fourth, because the names of the saints have a sort of romantic air about them, some land developers added a "San" to a name that sounded as if it should have one, such as "San" Quentin or "San" Ramon, neither of which places were originally named for saints. This tendency has carried over into street names; the city of Buena Park has half a dozen streets named for nonexistent saints, such as San Hacienda Circle and San Calvino Drive.

The early explorers, and the Franciscan Missionaries, believed that the saints for whom they named the landmarks and missions were genuine persons. Recent scholarship has sometimes cast doubt on the existence of some popular saints, such as St. Christopher; and sometimes it has suggested that a legend, such as that St. George slew a dragon, may not be true. But the 18th century was a more simple age, and people believed all the legends of the saints. They prayed to them, asked their intercession, and named their two most prized possessions, their children and their ranchos, in their honor. Small wonder, then, that so many places in California bear the names of saints.

INTRODUCTION

In preparing this volume for publication, several problems had to be taken into consideration. The first problem was one of inclusion or exclusion. Should the work be limited only to those place names beginning with the words "Saint," "San," or "Santa"? Or should it also include such place names as appear to have a religious connotation, some of which are indeed named for saints, such as Los Angeles or Soledad? And finally, should it also include place names which have a religious connotation, but which are not actually named for saints, such as Sacramento or Trinidad? The final decision was to include all such names.

The next problem was with the alphabetization of the names. After several different ways of listing them were tried, we thought it best to follow the system used by most guide books, by the ZIP Code directory, and by other sources, going word-by-word, and letter-by-letter within the word. Thus, "Sacramento" precedes "Saint ...," which in turn precedes "San ..." After the entries with "San" comes the "Santa's," and finally Trinidad and Ventura.

The third problem was the consideration of names that designate, not an inhabited place, but a hill, valley, creek, lagoon, rancho, or early land grant. There are about twenty of these. The decision was to include them all, but with a brief note, rather than a full entry, in an Appendix. A reference to this Appendix will be found at the appropriate places in the alphabetical sequence.

ACKNOWLEDGMENTS

The basic work for the study of the lives of the saints is the encyclopedic compilation whose brief title is *Acta Sanctorum*. This work was begun in Belgium in 1643, and has been continued through the centuries by a group known as the Bollandists. The compilation, now consisting of more than 85 folio volumes, is still incomplete.

From this collection of documents in their original languages, various scholars have abstracted and translated selected saint's lives and published them in various editions. Some typical compilations are:

> Sabine Baring-Gould, *Lives of the Saints*, Edinburgh, 1914; 16 volumes.
>
> Alban Butler, *Lives of the Saints*, London and New York, 1925-1938; 12 volumes.
>
> Frederick G. Holweck, *Biographical Dictionary of the Saints*, St. Louis, 1924. This is a one volume work, but it is now out of print and hard to obtain.

More recent compilations are as follows:

> *The Saints: a Concise Biographical Dictionary*, edited by John Coulson, New York, 1958.
>
> John J. Delaney, *Dictionary of Saints*, Garden City, N.Y., 1980. This is the most useful compilation currently available, and has been used extensively in the preparation of this booklet.

Additional information is to be found in the *New Catholic Encyclopedia* (1967), in 15 volumes.

For information regarding place names, the best work on the subject is:

> Erwin G. Gudde, *California Place Names*, Berkeley, Calif. (University of California Press, 1949; revised edition, 1969). Citations taken from this book have been used with the permission of the University of California Press.

Other useful sources of information about California place names are:

> *Historic Spots in California*, edited by William N. Abeloe, Stanford, Calif. (Stanford University Press, 3rd edition, 1966).
>
> James D. Hart, *A Companion to California*, New York (Oxford University Press, 1978).
>
> *The California Yearbook*, La Verne, Calif. (California Almanac Co., published at frequent intervals).

St. Joseph of Cupertino

ASUNCION: see Appendix.

CARMEL: see Appendix.

CATALINA: see under Santa Catalina.

CONCEPCION

This place name is derived from "la Purísima Concepción," one of the principal attributes of Our Lady; namely, that she was conceived in the womb of her mother, St. Anne, free from all stain of original sin. Hence the beautiful words of the poet Wordsworth, "Our tainted nature's solitary boast." The dogma of the Immaculate Conception was made an official part of the Church's teaching on December 8, 1854, though the festival and the doctrine date from a much earlier time.

Point Concepción was so named by the explorer Vizcaino, who reached that place on or about December 8, 1602. The later mission dedicated to la Purísima Concepción, in Santa Barbara County, was founded on the same date in 1797. A few other geographical features are also named either Purísima or Concepción, in different counties of the state.

Feast day: December 8.

CUPERTINO

·St. Joseph of Cupertino, in Italy, was a Franciscan mystic. He was permitted to enter the Franciscan Order only after serving some time as a servant in the local friary. Though no great scholar, he was at length ordained a priest. He became famous for his miracles, and especially for his ability to rise up from the ground while in a mystical trance, something he did some seventy times during his lifetime, always in the sight of reputable witnesses. He was troubled by the publicity surrounding his life, and tried in vain to live in obscurity, dying in 1663. He is the patron saint of aviators.

Cupertino in Santa Clara County owes its name to a creek (probably today's Stevens Creek) named for the saint by the Anza Expedition in 1776. A post office was established in 1882, and the city was incorporated in 1955.

Feast day: September 18.

Our Lady of Guadalupe

GUADALUPE

In December 1531, only a decade after the conquest of Mexico by Cortez and his men, an unlettered Mexican named Juan Diego, who spoke only his native Nahuatl, received five apparitions of Our Lady. She told him to get his bishop's permission to build a shrine in her honor on a small hill north of the Mexican capital. To convince the bishop she caused fresh roses to bloom in the winter, and her own image to appear miraculously on Juan's *tilma*, or peasant's cloak. The shrine was to be called "Guadalupe," but the exact origin of the name is uncertain. There was already a famous shrine of Our Lady of Guadalupe in Spain. Whether the bishop misunderstood a Nahuatl word with a similar sound, or whether the Virgin had directed the same name to be given in the New World, we shall never know. In any event, a shrine was built, and later a basilica, near the place of the apparitions, and devotion to Our Lady of Guadalupe soon became nationwide. The *tilma* and the image upon it are still preserved in a basilica at Tepayac, now part of Mexico City.

The name Guadalupe often occurs as a place name in California -- a river in Santa Clara County, named in 1776; and the city of Guadalupe in Santa Barbara County, incorporated in 1946, are only two examples.

Feast day: December 12.

JUNÍPERO Serra

Padre Junípero Serra was born in Petra, Majorca, in the Balearic Islands, in 1713. He entered the Franciscan Order in 1731, taking the name of Junípero, after the favorite companion of St. Francis, Brother Juniper. After studying and teaching at the University at Palma for several years, he volunteered for the North American mission field. He reached Mexico in 1749, and was soon assigned to the Sierra Gorda missions, far to the north of Mexico City. There he labored for eight years, before being recalled to the capital, to take up parish work and preaching. He was very successful in these occupations for nearly a decade. But events in Spain had their effect on the peaceful life of Fr. Serra. In 1767 King Charles III, yielding to political pressure and the anti-clerical spirit of the times, ordered all members of the Jesuit order to be expelled from all Spanish dominions, including Mexico. Fr. Serra, then 54 years of age, was told to ready himself to lead a group of Franciscans to take over the Jesuit missions in Baja California, and also to prepare to found new missions farther north. In 1769 the Sacred Expedition, as it was called, reached a place called Velicatá, still in Baja California, where the Jesuits had started to establish a mission, but had not had time to complete the work. Fr. Serra here founded his first mission, dedicating it to San Fernando, before proceeding on to San Diego, where he also founded one. Both of these events occurred in the summer of 1769. In 1770 he went by ship to Monterey and there founded Mission San Carlos. By the time of his death in 1784, seven more missions had been founded, either by him in person or under his direction. And the impetus that he gave, by his zeal, his holiness, and his wise guidance and leadership, resulted in the founding of a total of twenty-one missions in Alta California by the year 1823.

Fr. Serra was officially declared by the Pope to be "Venerable" on May 9, 1985. This is the first of three major steps in the lengthy process of Canonization. (For more information, see the Preface, above).

Junipero Serra Peak in the Santa Lucia Mountains (Monterey County) was officially named in 1906. Subsequently many streets, boulevards, hospitals, and other institutions have been named in honor of the Father President of the California Missions, though without the designation "San" in front of the name.

Church of Our Lady, Queen of the Angels

KINGS

This river in Kern County was named in honor of the Three Wise Men, or Kings, or Magi, who came bearing gifts for the infant Jesus in Bethlehem. In Spanish the wording is Los Santos Reyes, the Holy Kings. Though the three Magi have never been officially recognized as saints, the names that tradition has given them -- Balthasar, Caspar, and Melchior -- have occasionally been bestowed on children, in the same manner as saints' names. Examples are Balthasar, Margave of Thuringia (1381-1406); Lt. Caspar Collins (died in 1865), for whom Casper, Wyoming was named; and Melchior Cano (1509-1560), a famous Spanish theologian. There is also a recent St. Caspar, canonized in 1954. So perhaps the Three Wise Men have been popularly, if not officially, recognized as saints.

The Kings River was named in 1805. Kingston and Kingsburg, on or near the river, have derived their names from it. Kings County was formed in 1893.

Feast day: January 6 (the feast of the Epiphany); also July 23.

LOS ANGELES

Today's city of Los Angeles was called "El Pueblo de la Reina de Los Angeles" in official documents some years before it actually existed. It was founded on September 4, 1781, by military personnel from Mission San Gabriel who apportioned small lots to the new settlers, acting on orders of the Governor. The patron saint of the new pueblo was Nuestra Señora (Our Lady, the Virgin Mary), under one of her many titles, Queen of the Angels. This stemmed from the fact that Fr. Crespí, chaplain and diarist of the 1769 Portolá Expedition, gave the name Porciúncula to the nearby river, because they arrived on August 2, the day of the Porciúncula Indulgence. (Note: the word Porciúncula (in Italian, Porziuncula) refers to an abandoned chapel, named "Our Lady of the Angels," where St. Francis had lived as a young man. He called it his "little portion" of land, his only worldly possession. Later an indulgence (a spiritual benefit) was granted by the Pope to the faithful who visisted this shrine and prayed there. Still later this benefit, called the Porciúncula Indulgence, was extended to any of the faithful who visited and prayed in a Franciscan church, anywhere in the world, on that day each year).

Fr. Crespí, recalling that St. Francis' beloved little chapel had been named for Our Lady of the Angels, then called the entire region "el Río y Valle de Nuestra Señora del los Angeles de la Porciúncula," and predicted that "in time to come a very large and rich mission" might be built in that area.

Feast day (the Porciúncula Indulgence): August 2.

MADONNA: see Appendix.

State Capitol, Sacramento

MERCED

This is another instance, like Los Angeles, Soledad, and others, of a place name in honor of Our Lady, in this case Our Lady of Mercy. The meaning is, not mercy in the sense of sparing an adversary, but rather in the sense of forgiveness of sins; for it is Catholic doctrine that Our Lady can intercede with her son, Jesus Christ, to ask forgiveness for the sins of mortal man.

Lake Merced in San Francisco was first named in September 1775. The Merced River was first so named by Gabriel Moraga in September 1806. The county of Merced was created in 1855, and named after its principal river. The city was laid out when the railroad came through in 1872. A few other geographical sites also bear the name; Merced Grove of big trees, Merced Lake, and so on. All have the same basic origin.

There is no specific feast day for Our Lady of Mercy. (See under Santa Maria for other feasts).

NATIVIDAD: see Appendix.

REFUGIO: see Appendix.

SACRAMENTO

The Spanish word for the Most Holy Sacrament often occurs in Spanish-American nomenclature. It refers to the belief of Catholics (and others) that the priest at the altar, during the most solemn part of the Mass, repeats the word used by Christ at the Last Supper, the day before he died on the cross. At these words, "This is my body ..." and "This is my blood ...," the bread and wine on the altar are transubstantiated (their substance is changed) into the body and blood of Christ. This is the essence of the Most Holy Sacrament referred to by the pious Spanish explorers.

The name of the present state capital was first applied to the Sacramento River by Gabriel Moraga in 1808, though he may have used it for what we now call the Feather River, one of its tributaries. But in 1817 Fr. Duran of Mission San José made a trip up the larger river, calling the entire body of water El Río del Sacramento, which permanently fixed the name.

Feast day: Corpus Christi, a movable feast, eleven days after Pentecost.

St. George

Saint GEORGE

St. George is the patron saint of England, and of some half-dozen other countries too, and he is also held in high esteem in the Orthodox churches of the East. He probably did not slay any dragon; this is a romantic fiction. However, there was no doubt a man named George (the name, by the way, means "farmer" or "agriculturist") who was a soldier in the Imperial Army, and he did suffer martyrdom about 303, during the reign of Diocletian. But all else is legend.

The name survives in California in several maritime features (channel, cape, reef, etc.) in Del Norte County, all bestowed by the Englishman Vancouver in 1792, in honor of the patron saint of England. Vancouver probably did not know that Vizcaino had been there before him, and had named the point Cabo Blanco de San Sebastián in 1603.

Feast day: April 23.

Saint HELENA

St. Helen was the mother of the Emperor Constantine, who in 313 issued the famous Edict of Milan, effectively putting an end to nearly 300 years of persecution of the Christian religion. Helen soon after this went to Palestine, where she discovered the True Cross on which Christ had died. She also built churches, and spent her time and money administering to the sick, the poor, and to prisoners.

Mount St. Helena in Sonoma County was probably so named by the personnel of a Russian ship named "St. Helena" as it was approaching the shore, from which distance the peak is clearly visible. This was about 1840. (Earlier land grants in the vicinity merely used the names of the local tribes). There is a romantic story that a Russian Princess Helena climbed the mountain and named it in honor of her patron saint, but this is only a legend. The town of St. Helena in nearby Napa County was so named (post office, 1858) because of its fine view of the mountain.

Feast day: August 18.

San AGUSTIN: see Appendix.

San ANDREAS

St. Andrew was the first person chosen by Christ to become one of his apostles. He was the son of a man named John, a commercial fisherman on the Sea of Galilee; he had a brother named Simon who, later renamed Peter, became the first Pope of the Roman Catholic Church. Andrew was martyred at Patras in northern Greece, being suspended (according to a much later legend) from a cross with arms and legs extended; hence the familiar X-shaped Cross of St. Andrew. He is regarded as the patron saint of Scotland and of Russia, though he probably never visited either of these countries.

In California his name is associated with earthquakes, because the great earthquake that devastated the Bay Area in 1906 was on a fault running through the San Andreas Valley of San Mateo County. The name San Andrés was first given to that valley on November 30, 1774, by Fr. Palou. But in 1875, when the first dam was built in the valley, the spelling San Andreas crept into the documents, and it has been spelled that way ever since. There is also a community of San Andreas in the gold country, the county seat of Calaveras County, first so named about 1848.

Feast day: November 30.

Mission San Antonio

San ANSELMO

St. Anselm was an 11th century Benedictine monk, who, though born in Italy, became abbot of the French monastery of Bec. There was an English branch of this monastery near London, and while on an official visit there he was persuaded to become Archbishop of Canterbury. In this position he defended the rights of the Church against two English kings, as well as preaching against heresy and social injustice. He is equally famous for his success in incorporating Aristotle's metaphysics into Christian theology. He was likewise an outstanding theologian, and his work "Why Did God Become Man?" was a standard text for several hundred years.

The city of San Anselmo in Marin County (incorporated 1894) was probably not named directly for St. Anselm, but rather for a local Indian who had been given this name in baptism. The place name first appeared in 1840, without the "San." That was added later, probably by real estate developers.

Feast day: April 21.

San ANTONIO

St. Anthony of Padua is one of the most popular saints of today, since he is appealed to by pious people whenever they lose something. "A quick prayer to St. Anthony" is believed to help find missing car keys, screwdrivers, children's toys, or anything at all. The saint was born in Portugal, in 1195, and was named Ferdinand. On entering the Franciscan Order, after his ordination to the priesthood, he took the name Anthony. Afterwards he went to Italy, becoming a famous preacher and residing mostly in Padua, where he died from overwork at the age of 36.

Mission San Antonio, founded by Fr. Serra in 1771, is a center of Franciscan religious life, and is visited by thousands of tourists every year. It is adjacent to, but not part of, the Hunter Liggett Military Reservation in Monterey County. The name is also commemorated in Mt. San Antonio ("Old Baldy"), the highest peak of the San Gabriel Mountains of Southern California. That name was originally bestowed by another Franciscan explorer, Francisco Garcés, in 1774.

Feast day: June 13.

San ARDO

This is a small settlement in the Salinas Valley, in Monterey County. It is not named for any saint. Erwin Gudde, in his book *California Place Names*, says that originally (1886) the railroad station and the town were called San Bernardo, after a nearby ranch. But the Post Office Department objected, fearing confusion with San Bernardino down south. So they chopped off the "Bern" and created an instant saint, San Ardo. However, there actually was a Saint Ardo, though it is unlikely that any Spaniard, or Mexican, or railroad official of the 18th or 19th centuries ever heard of him. He was a Benedictine abbot of Aniane in Languedoc, Southern France, in the early 9th century. His proper name was Smaragdus, but he took the name Ardo upon entering his religious order. He was director of the monastery-school of Aniane, which became one of the best-known in all Languedoc.

Feast day: March 7.

St. Benedict

San BENANCIO: see Appendix.

San BENITO

St. Benedict was born in Nursia, Italy, about 480. Disgusted by the sinfulness of city life, Benedict tried to live a solitary life in the nearby mountains, but his piety became famous, and some monks asked him to be their Abbot. He complied, and soon had twelve monasteries under his leadership. For these, and later foundations, he wrote explicit rules of conduct, the basic principle being "work and pray." The Benedictine Order had a profound influence on Europe for about 600 years, civilizing barbaric tribes, teaching them to till the land, and bringing order and law to regions devastated by warfare. Their monasteries served as reservoirs of learning, and their libraries preserved the best of classical literature in the ages before the invention of printing.

The name, San Benito, was bestowed on a creek now within the San Benito County in 1772. The county itself was created in 1874, from a portion of Monterey County.

Feast day: March 21.

San BERNARBE: see Appendix.

San BERNARDINO

St. Bernardine of Siena (1380-1444) was orphaned at an early age, and was raised by a pious aunt. He entered the Franciscan Order shortly after age 20, and later became an eloquent preacher, traveling all over Italy. Since he denounced the evils of his time he soon made enemies, who brought charges against him. He was cleared of these by the Pope, who offered to consecrate him a bishop. This he declined, but at about age 30 he accepted the position of Vicar-General of his Order. He built up the Observantine Friars from a membership of about 300 to over 4000, and is termed a "second founder," after St. Francis.

San Bernardino is not the earliest, but the best known, place name in California honoring this saint. It was originally a rancho of Mission San Gabriel (about 1810), then, in 1819, an *asistencia* (an outlying branch of a mission), and seems to have been continuously inhabited since that time. The American explorer Jedediah Smith and his men passed through the rancho in 1826. The present city dates from a Mormon colony founded in 1851. The county was established in 1853, and the city was incorporated in 1869.

Feast day: May 20.

Mission San Carlos, Carmel

San BRUNO

St. Bruno was born of a prominent Cologne family in 1030, went to the best schools there and in Rheims, and eventually became a priest and professor at the college there, as well as Chancellor of the diocese of Rheims. Forced to leave after his denunciation of an unsavory but popular character in that city, he chose an eremetical life (one in which pious men lived in separate dwellings, rather than in a community under the guidance of an Abbot, as the Benedictines did). He was given some land in the Alps, called La Grande Chartreuse, where he and some followers founded the Carthusian Order of hermits, adapting St. Benedict's Rule to their way of life. This was about 1084. St. Bruno died in 1090.

San Bruno, in San Mateo County, has been a place name in that area since Fr. Palou applied the name, late in 1774, to a small creek running down from the San Bruno Mountain of today. The city was incorporated in 1914.

Feast day: October 6.

San BUENAVENTURA: see under Ventura, below.

San CAJETANO: see Appendix.

San CARLOS

St. Charles Borromeo was born of a noble Lombard family in their castle home on Lago Maggiore, in 1538. When his uncle was elected Pope in 1559, young Charles was summoned to Rome, made a lay-Cardinal and Administrator of the diocese of Milan, as well as Papal Secretary of State. When the heir to the headship of the Borromeo family died, and Charles was next in line to inherit, he renounced the inheritance. Subsequently he was ordained a priest, and later consecrated bishop of Milan. In 1569, he was the victim of an assassination attack by some members of a dissolute religious order he was trying to reform. He survived the attack, lived a devout life, and was a patron of the arts until his death in November 1584.

The mission founded at Monterey in 1770 by Fr. Serra was named for him, but later the mission was transferred to Carmel Valley, and is now popularly known as the Carmel Mission. The city of San Carlos in San Mateo County was not named until 1887, though it was probably named indirectly for St. Charles Borromeo.

Feast day: November 4.

San CARPOFORO: see Appendix.

Mission San Diego

San CLEMENTE

St. Clement was the third Pope of the Roman Church, from about 88 to 97, in which year he was sent into exile in the Crimea by the emperor Trajan, dying there about the year 100. Unreliable legends have grown up around his name, such as that he caused a well to spring up for his thirsty fellow-exiles in the Crimea.

The name San Clemente was given by Vizcaino to the island (now a Navy base) south of Catalina Island on November 25, 1602. It may have been wishful thinking on his part. His chaplains had celebrated the feast of San Clemente only two days earlier, and Vizcaino may have wished the saint to perform another miracle and produce fresh water for his men on that somewhat barren island. The resort community of San Clemente in Orange County was named after the island.

Feast day: November 23.

San DIEGITO: a diminutive form of San Diego.

San DIEGO

The English-language version of this name causes some difficulty. Actually, Diego was an early Spanish form of James, though historically the spelling "Santiago" has been used as a battle-cry, for St. James, the patron saint of Spain. San Diego de Alcalá de Henares (1400-1463), for whom the city of San Diego was named, was a Franciscan lay brother, who lived a holy life as a missionary helper in the Canary Islands. Later he lived in Alcalá, with a reputation for holiness and miracles. The Latin form of his name is Didacus.

The harbor of San Diego was first visited by Cabrillo in 1542 and named San Miguel. Vizcaino, anchoring there on November 10, 1602, renamed the place San Diego in honor of his flagship (and because San Diego's feast day was only three days later). When Fr. Serra came to found a mission there he knew that the harbor had already been named, and for a Franciscan saint, so he chose that name for the mission.

Feast day: November 13.

San DIMAS

St. Dismas is the legendary name of one the two thieves crucified with Christ on Calvary. Another name for him is "the Good Thief." There is a pious legend to the effect that these two robbers held up Mary and Joseph while on their way to Egypt, when they fled with their child Jesus to escape the wrath of Herod. The legend goes on to say that the child Jesus predicted that the two of them would be apprehended in later life, and would die with him on the cross; but that one of them, Dismas, who bribed his companion to leave the Holy Family unmolested, would be saved and would go with him into Paradise.

San Dimas in Los Angeles County was laid out and named in 1886/87. Another story relates that Ygnacio Palomares, the former owner of the land, selected the name because of some renegade Indians who had stolen his cattle, but this too is probably just a story.

Feast day: March 25.

St. Francis of Assisi

San (or Santo) DOMINGO: see Appendix.

San ELIJO: see Appendix.

San EMIGDIO: see Appendix.

San FELIPE: see Appendix.

San FERNANDO

St. Ferdinand was King Ferdinand III of Castile and Leon, reigning from 1217 to 1252. He was a valiant enemy of the Moors, whose capital cities of Cordova and Sevilla he captured. He forced the king of Granada to do homage to him, but was unable to capture the city, leaving that to a later Ferdinand (and Isabella) to accomplish in 1492. He was also a vigorous opponent of heresies, and it was probably for this, rather than for his military exploits, that he was canonized by the Church in 1671. His body lies in state in a beautiful chapel behind the high altar in the cathedral of Sevilla.

The famous San Fernando Valley, now almost entirely within the city limits of Los Angeles, takes its name from Mission San Fernando, founded in 1797; and the separate city of San Fernando was laid out in 1874, close by the old mission property.

Feast day: May 30.

San FRANCISCO

St. Francis of Assisi was named John by his mother at birth (1181), but when his father returned from a business trip to France he insisted that the boy's name be changed to Francis. (Other stories say that he was named "Francis" because as a young dandy he affected French airs and French words in his conversation). After a series of adventures as a young man, Francis had a vision and was converted to a more sober way of life about 1205/06. He went on a pilgrimage to Rome; then, returning to Assisi, he set himself up as a hermit in an abandoned chapel which he called his Porziuncula (in Spanish Porciúncula), his "little portion" of land. Preaching poverty and repentance, he founded the Franciscan Order of friars ("brethren"), and his Order soon spread throughout Christendom. He died in 1226, a few years after he built the first "Christmas crib," thereby establishing a custom at Christmas that has become worldwide.

The city by the Golden Gate was established as a mission and presidio in 1776, though the name, applied to headlands and other natural features, appears on maps as early as 1590.

Feast day: October 4.

Mission San Gabriel

San GABRIEL

The Archangel Gabriel is not strictly a saint, and having never been a human being, does not have a "life" to be narrated. He is mentioned in the Bible as being "one of the seven who stand before God." Gabriel's name means, approximately, "hero of God," and he was sent frequently from heaven to foretell human events. His best known visit is the one he made to Nazareth in Palestine, when he announced to the young girl Mary that she was to become the Mother of God. This is celebrated as the feast of the Annunciation, on March 25, exactly nine months prior to Christmas.

San Gabriel Mission was founded on September 8, 1774. The present city of San Gabriel had its origins in the settlements that grew up around the mission following secularization in the 1830's, and has been a continuous area of population since that time. Its post office was established in 1854, and it was incorporated in 1913.

Feast day: historically March 24; recently changed to September 29.

San GERONIMO

St. Jerome was born about 340, in Stridon, northern Dalmatia, a region which today is part of Yugoslavia. A pagan, he studied at Rome the great Greek and Roman classics, but was baptized at age 20, and turned to studying religious authors. Wishing to live a secluded life, he went first to a deserted region of Syria, near Chalcis, about fifty miles southeast of Antioch. Here he was surrounded, as he writes in one of his letters, by "scorpions and wild beasts." But the legend that he tamed a lion, which lay at his feet while he wrote, merely demonstrates medieval Europe's ignorance of geography. Jerome's lasting fame is his translation of the the whole Bible, from Hebrew, Aramaic, and Greek into what was then the speech of the common people, Latin. His version, called the "Vulgate," because it was written in the common, or vulgar, tongue, remained the standard text of the Bible for over 1500 years.

There is a small community in Marin County that bears this name. It was the name of a railroad station in 1875, and there has been a post office there since 1898.

Feast day: September 30.

San GORGONIO: see Appendix.

San GREGORIO

St. Gregory the Great (540-604) was born and educated in Rome, and at the age of about 30 was made Prefect of that city. A few years later he left public life and founded a monastery on his own property, under the Rule of St. Benedict. Later ordained, and made a cardinal, he went as papal nuncio to Byzantium in 579, and was there six years. Recalled to Rome, he was again allowed to enter a monastery, but in 590 he was elected Pope. He made many reforms in the Church and was responsible for the conversion of England, by sending St. Augustine and forty monks to Canterbury. He is at least partly responsible for the body of ecclesiastical music we call the Gregorian chant.

The community of San Gregorio, near the coast in San Mateo County, was first visited by the men of the Portolá Expedition, about October 25/26, 1769. The name, Arroyo de San Gregorio, first appears on a map in 1839, and the post office dates from the 1870's.

Feast day: March 12 (some recent calendars give September 3).

[21]

Mount San Jacinto, near Palm Springs

San JACINTO

St. Hyacinth's birthplace seems to be disputed between German and Polish Silesia, but it was probably near Breslau, in Germany. Joining the newly founded Dominican Order of friars about 1216, he was sent with a group of his brethren into Poland, where he preached and established several Dominican friaries. He has been named the Apostle of Poland, though he also preached in Prussia and Lithuania, and even as far away as Scandinavia. He worked many miracles during his lifetime, and died on August 17, 1257.

The famous Mount San Jacinto, behind Palm Springs, was probably not so named until about 1859. The name is derived from a cattle rancho of Mission San Luis Rey, established in 1821. There has been a post office with the same name near the foot of the mountain since 1870, and the city of San Jacinto in Riverside County was incorporated in 1880.

Feast day: August 17.

San JOAQUIN

St. Joachim is revered throughout Christendom as the father of the Virgin Mary. The legend has it that he and his wife Anne, being childless after some years of marriage, prayed to the Lord to bless their union, the resulting child being the Virgin Mary. Nothing else is known or related about the life of St. Joachim, but his name has been bestowed upon young Spaniards for many centuries.

The famous San Joaquin Valley of Central California takes its name from its principal river, which in turn was named by Gabriel Moraga in 1813 in honor of his father, José Joaquín Moraga, who was *Comandante* at San Francisco until his death in 1785. The name has been also applied to a county, and to various hills and peaks, as well as to the city of San Joaquin in Fresno County. That city has had a post office since 1915, and was incorporated in 1920.

Feast day: July 26, celebrated along with his wife, St. Anne. (It was previously celebrated on August 16, and it also appears in some calendars on March 20).

San JOSE

St. Joseph is one of the most beloved saints of all time. A carpenter, engaged to a young girl of Nazareth named Mary, he had to contend with what must have been an embarrassing situation when she was found to be pregnant during their engagement, though he knew himself to be innocent. But he was reassured by an angel in a dream, who told him that "the child that shall be born of her shall be called the Son of God," and that the child had been conceived, not by any mortal man, but by the Holy Spirit. Joseph believed the angel, took Mary for his wife, shielded her from malicious gossip, and finally took her with him, in obedience to Roman law, to his ancestral home, Bethlehem, to be properly registered there as a taxpayer. There, at what we now call Christmas time, her son was born and was named Jesus.

The city of San Jose, in Santa Clara County, takes its origin from a pueblo, founded in 1777, the first civic community to be established in California. Twenty years later, Mission San Jose in Alameda County, at some distance from the pueblo, was founded. Both are named for the same saint, the foster father of Our Lord.

Feast day: March 19.

Mission San Juan Capistrano

San JUAN BAUTISTA

St. John the Baptist was a close relative of Jesus, his mother Elizabeth being a "kinswoman" of Mary of Nazareth. John was about six months older than Jesus. While preaching repentance and baptizing along the River Jordan, he denounced the sinful life of King Herod, who had married Herodias, the wife of his half-brother Philip. Herod had John arrested and imprisoned. During a festival in his palace, Salome, daughter of Herodias, danced before the king and pleased him. Infatuated, Herod promised her anything she desired. Her mother urged her to ask for the head of John the Baptist, and Herod, unwilling but ashamed to break his work before his courtiers, ordered the execution.

Mission San Juan Bautista in San Benito County was founded only a few days after Mission San Jose, in 1797. A community grew up around the mission, though the latter was abandoned after 1836, and not restored until 1884. The city was incorporated in 1896.

Feast day: June 24 and August 29.

San JUAN CAPISTRANO

This St. John was born in the Italian town of Capistrano, Province of Abruzzi, in the year 1386. He was a man of some local importance, and for a while was governor of the city of Perugia. But during a period of imprisonment, when he happened to be on the losing side in a civil war, he felt a call to a more spiritual life. At age 30 he joined the Franciscans, and after a while became a leader of the Observantine branch of that Order, along with St. Bernardine of Siena. He preached repentance in many countries of Europe until 1453; after that he devoted himself to persuading his fellow Christians to resist the Turks, who were then threatening all of Europe. To this end he even led a wing of the army at the Battle of Belgrade (1456), which effectively put an end to land invasions of Europe by the Turks. He died shortly afterwards, probably of the plague.

Mission San Juan Capistrano was founded by Fr. Serra in November 1776. The present city has had a post office since 1867, but under the name Capistrano. The full name was restored in 1905.

Feast day: March 28.

San JULIAN: see Appendix.

San LEANDRO

St. Leander (534-600) was a member of a famous Spanish family of Cartagena, being the elder brother of the great St. Isidore of Seville. (See under San Ysidro, below). Leander helped in the education of his younger brother, and when he (Leander), retired from his position as Archbishop of Seville, it was his brother Isidore who was chosen to succeed him. St. Leander is primarily responsible for restoring Spain to strict Catholicism, after it had become seriously infected by the heresy of Arianism. It was he who ordered the reading of the Nicene Creed during the liturgy of the Mass, a practice still followed today. He was a close friend of St. Gregory the Great, and it was at his suggestion that Gregory published his great work, the *Moralia,* originally a series of sermons based on the Book of Job.

The city of San Leandro was laid out in 1855, taking its name from a nearby creek. That creek was named for St. Leander as early as 1828, but by whom it is now impossible to discover.

Feast day: February 27.

St. Louis, Bishop of Toulouse

San LORENZO

St. Lawrence was born, according to tradition, at Huesca in northern Spain, probably about 210 or 215. He went to Rome, and was made a deacon (i.e., a financial administrator) for Pope Sixtus II (257-258). When the Emperor Valerian heard rumors that the Christians possessed "hidden treasures," he ordered Lawrence to deliver them up. The saint did so, bringing before the Emperor some sick, diseased, and lame beggars to whom he had been distributing alms, saying "These are our treasures." Angered at this, the Emperor ordered a huge griddle to be prepared and heated with coals, upon which St. Lawrence was stretched out and burned to death. During the later years of 1563 to 1584, King Philip II of Spain built a huge mausoleum and monastery in honor of St. Lawrence, called El Escorial, in the mountains north of Madrid.

The name San Lorenzo occurs in two principal places in California; as a river in Santa Cruz County, so named in 1769; and as a small community in Alameda County, just north of San Leandro, where a creek was so named in 1772.

Feast day: August 10.

San LUCAS

St. Luke was one of the four evangelists (writers of a Gospel). Because of the medical details he gives in writing about the miracles of Christ, and because of his excellent Greek style, it is probable that he was an educated man, perhaps a physician. He may have studied at the university in Tarsus, and may have known St. Paul (then called Saul). Later in life he became Paul's companion, traveling with him to Rome. There wrote his Gospel, from about 61 to 70. This was the period of the persecution of Nero, when both Saints Peter and Paul were martyred. But Luke seems to have avoided arrest, and managed to get away to Greece. He died there at age 84.

The name San Lucas was applied to a land grant in the central part of the Salinas Valley in 1842, and when the railroad came through in 1886, the name was given to a station. The community, located in Monterey County, has had a post office since 1892.

Feast day: October 18.

San LUIS (GONZAGA): see Appendix.

San LUIS OBISPO

St. Louis, Bishop of Toulouse in France (1274-1297), was the second son of Charles II, Duke of Anjou and King of Naples. Another St. Louis, King of France, was his great-uncle. His father, Charles, was captured in a naval battle by the King of Aragon, and was imprisoned from 1284 to 1288. One of the conditions of his eventual release was that he leave his young son Louis as hostage in Barcelona. The lad was educated there by the Franciscans; he entered their Order at age 18. Soon afterwards he was ordained, and in 1295 was made bishop of Toulouse, not far from the Aragon border. Noted for his piety and his charities, he died in 1297, at the age of only 23. His body was brought back to Spain for burial in Valencia.

Mission San Luis Obispo was founded by Fr. Serra in 1772. He and his companions did arrive in the area on the saint's feast day, but Fr. Serra seems to have decided on the name some time earlier.

Feast day: August 19.

Mission San Luis Rey

San LUIS·REY

St. Louis, King of France (1214-1270), is one of the few kings ever to be declared a saint. His mother, the pious Blanche of Castile, brought him up to be a God-fearing young man. He married a daughter of a Count of Provence, and they had a large family. He went on two Crusades, the first of which was a disaster, for he was captured and had to be ransomed. On his second Crusade, in 1270, he got only as far as Tunis, where he contracted typhoid fever and died. He was renowned for piety, even asceticism, as well as for honesty in his government, and for his support of the rights of the oppressed and the unfortunate. He was declared a saint in 1297, barely a quarter of a century after his death.

Mission San Luis Rey was not founded until 1798 (and the name personally chosen by the Viceroy), though the area had been recommended for a mission, and so named, as early as 1769.

Feast day: August 25.

San MARCOS

St. Mark was one of the four evangelists (those who wrote a Gospel). He was a disciple of St. Peter, and his Gospel often mentions Peter, and to some extent reflects his teachings. He went on two journeys with him, and was with him in Rome about the year 61. There he most likely wrote his Gospel. There is a legend that he was later made bishop of Alexandria, and was martyred there. His body was supposedly stolen by Venetian merchants and brought from Alexandria to Venice in 829, the saint's body being packed in a casket labeled "pork," so that the Saracen port officials (who religiously avoided any contact with the flesh of pigs) would not investigate the contents. Not surprisingly, he is the patron saint of Venice.

The city of San Marcos in San Diego County, incorporated in 1963, goes back as a place name at least to a rancho in 1835, and to a valley so named in 1797. San Marcos Pass in Santa Barbara County also takes its name from a nearby rancho, so named in 1817.

Feast day: April 25.

San MARIN: see Appendix.

San MARINO

St. Marinus was a 4th century stonemason of Dalmatia, a region of modern-day Yugoslavia. Following his calling, he went to work in some quarries in Italy, where he was converted to a religious way of life by the piety of some Christians who were condemned to work as slaves in the quarries. Later, a demented woman pursued him, claiming he was her husband who had deserted her. To escape this problem he fled to the mountains of central Italy, and became a hermit. The town and later republic of San Marino derive their name from this legendary saint.

San Marino, near Pasadena in Los Angeles County, obtained its name as recently as 1878, after an estate of that name in Maryland, which in turn had been named after San Marino in Italy.

Feast day: September 4.

Mission San Miguel

San MARTIN

There are several saints named Martin, but the most likely one here is St. Martin of Tours (316-397). Born in (today's) Hungary, of pagan parents, he was taken by them at an early age to Pavia in Italy. There, as the son of an army officer, he too was inducted into the army. By this time he had become a Christian. At Amiens in France occurred the incident so often painted, when he cut his warm military cloak in two and gave half of it to a beggar. Later that night Martin had a vision of Christ wearing the donated half of the cloak. Permitted to resign his commission on religious grounds, he became a hermit; later he was ordained and made bishop of Tours, on the basis of his reputation for holiness and miracles. He spent his remaining years in asceticism as well as in the administration of his diocese.

The community of San Martín in Santa Clara County was first named by Martin Murphy, an Irish Catholic, who settled nearby in 1844. Cape San Martín in Monterey County, however, was so named by Cabrillo in 1542.

Feast day: November 11.

San MATEO

St. Matthew was one of the four evangelists (those who wrote a Gospel). In fact his Gospel is always listed first, and it is the only one most likely written in Aramaic, the language Jesus spoke, rather than in Greek (though only Greek translations survive). He was a tax collector at Capharnaum when he heeded Christ's call to be an apostle. His name was sometimes confused with that of Matthias, and it is impossible to say where he went to preach the gospel after the Resurrection. There is a strong tradition that he was martyred some time after the year 70.

San Mateo County and City derive their names from a creek in the area so named by Fr. Font in 1772. Later there was a sheep ranch there, an adjunct to Mission Dolores. The county was created in 1856 and the city incorporated in 1896.

Feast day: September 21.

San MIGUEL

St. Michael is "one of the seven who stand before God," and is one of only three archangels named in the Bible. He is represented in art as holding a drawn sword with the wording "Quis ut Deus" (Who is Like unto God) inscribed on it. In the book of Revelations (Apocalypse) St. John wrote that he saw "Michael and his angels doing battle with the dragon; and the dragon was cast out, the old serpent called the Devil ..."

The oldest place named for St. Michael in California is one of the Channel Islands off Santa Barbara, discovered by Cabrillo in 1542, but given a different name at that time, and additional different names by other explorers until 1790, when the name San Miguel was definitely fixed. Mission San Miguel in San Luis Obispo County was founded in 1797, and the name was assigned to the new railroad station in 1886 and to a post office in 1887. San Miguel was also the name of several early land grants.

Feast day: September 29.

St. Nicholas (today's "Santa Claus")

San NICOLAS

St. Nicholas is the prototype of our popular Santa Claus. He was Bishop of Myra, in ancient Lycia, part of today's Turkey, dying there some time in the 4th century. In the 11th century his relics were brought to Bari, in southern Italy. Stories grew up around him; such as that he once provided dowries for three girls from poor families. From these and other legends he obtained a reputation as a giver of gifts, and his image in northern, non-Catholic Europe shifted from that of a bishop to that of a benevolent old man. The Dutch of New Amsterdam (now New York) called him, in their language, "Santa Claus," and shifted his festival from early December to Christmas Eve.

San Nicolás Island, 75 miles south of Ventura, is famous as the "Island of the Blue Dolphins." In 1835, raids by sea-otter hunters, in reality little more than pirates, had decimated the native Indians. Unable to protect them, the government ordered the island evacuated. One woman, believing that her child was still on the island, jumped from the boat and swam ashore. She lived alone for 18 years, until rescued by George Nidever in 1853. She is buried in the mission garden in Santa Barbara.

Feast day: December 6.

San ONOFRE

St. Onuphrius was a hermit living about the year 400 in the desert region beyond the River Nile, in the general area of the modern city of Luxor. A holy man, he had a premonition of his own death. One time a famous abbot, St. Paphnutius, unsure of his true vocation in life, came to visit him. That night St. Onuphrius died, and Paphnutius buried him in a cave, the site of which disappeared the next day, as if to tell St. Paphnutius that he was not to remain a hermit, but to return to the city and do the will of God there.

The name San Onofre was first applied to a rancho of Mission San Juan Capistrano in 1828. When the Santa Fe Railroad ran a line from Los Angeles to Oceanside in the late 1880's a station was so named. Today it is best known as the site of the experimental nuclear power station close to the main highway between Los Angeles and San Diego.

Feast day: June 12.

San PABLO

St. Paul, the greatest of all teachers of the doctrines of Christ, was born of Jewish parents in Tarsus, and was probably about ten years younger than Jesus. Educated by the great rabbi Gamaliel in Jerusalem, Saul, as he was then called, became a strictly orthodox scholar, and vehemently attacked the new sect of Christians. While riding between Jerusalem and Damascus he was struck down from his horse by an angel, and saw in a vision the risen Christ. Half-blinded by the vision, he made his way to a friendly house in Damascus, and was there baptized. His subsequent journeys, shipwrecks, and letters are all well known. He was martyred at Rome during the time of Nero, some time between 64 and 67.

The earliest of the many places and natural features in California named for him is the Punta de San Pablo, opposite to the Punta de San Pedro, in northern California, the two names being bestowed in 1811. Later the name was applied to the whole San Pablo Bay, and about 1850 to the city of San Pablo, just north of Richmond in Contra Costa County.

Feast day (shared with St. Peter): June 29.

St. Peter

San PASQUAL

There are several saints named Paschal, but the one for whom the area of the battlefield between the Californios and the Americans in 1840 was named was probably a Franciscan lay brother called Paschal Baylon (1540-1592), born in Aragon during the Paschal season -- hence his name. A devout youth, he entered the Observantine Order of the Franciscans (the more strict observance of the Rule) about 1560. He was sent on some diplomatic missions but preferred the simpler life of a humble lay brother. After his death many miracles were recorded through his intercession. He was canonized in 1640.

The site of the famous battle of San Pasqual (also spelled Pascual) was originally a ranchería or village of Christian Indians under the jurisdiction of Mission San Diego. It changed hands several times after secularization of the missions, and is now a State Historic Monument, a few miles east of Escondido.

Feast day: May 17.

San PEDRO

St. Peter, the first Pope, the brother of Andrew, was the son of a commercial fisherman named John, who ran a boat on the Sea of Galilee. His original name was Simon. Called by Christ to join him in his preaching, he soon became a leader among the apostles. He was with Jesus during most of the latter's public life, witnessed miracles, and himself walked miraculously upon the water. Christ changed his name to Peter (a rock) when he formally founded his Church, telling Peter that he was to be the principal leader of that Church after the Crucifixion. His courage failed him the night of Christ's arrest, and he denied that he ever knew Jesus. Later he became a fearless preacher, and after establishing himself in Rome was martyred there, some time between 64 and 67.

Though St. Peter of the New Testament is better known than any other, it is possible that the area of the Los Angeles harbor of today was first named, by Vizcaino on November 16, 1602, in honor of an Egyptian bishop (died 311) named Peter, whose feast it was that day.

Feast day of St. Peter the Apostle: June 29, shared with St. Paul.

San QUENTIN

St. Quentin (also called Quintinus) was an early Roman martyr. According to legend he resigned his army commission after being converted to Christianity, and went with some companions to preach the gospel in Gaul (France), settling at Amiens in Picardy. He was eventually arrested there, and tortured. Later he was taken to a Roman city in the Vermandois district, afterwards named Saint-Quentin in his honor, and there beheaded, about the year 287.

San Quentin in Marin County is now famous as the site of a prison. The point of land on which it stands was originally named Quentin, because a notorious Indian thief or rebel of that name was captured there, in 1824. Later the name was used for various land grants, but the word "San" was not added until after 1850. However, a formerly existing point of land on the San Francisco side of the Bay was definitely called Punta de San Quentin, about 1839; but due to reconstruction of the coast line, with small bays being filled in, the point has disappeared.

Feast day: October 31.

The Archangel Rafael descending to earth

San RAFAEL

The archangel Raphael is "one of the seven who stand before God," as the Bible says; but we know the names of only three of them, Gabriel, Michael, and Raphael. The name means "God heals," and Raphael is the angel sent by God to look after a young man, Tobias, on a long journey. The angel later cures the father of Tobias of his blindness. All of this is narrated in one of the books of the Old Testament, called "Tobias." This book formed part of the Vulgate edition of the Bible when it was translated into Latin by St. Jerome (see under San Geronimo, above) at the end of the 4th century, and it has remained in Catholic bibles to this day.

Mission San Rafael was founded as an *asistencia* (an outlying branch) of Mission Dolores in San Francisco in 1817. It was dedicated to the "healing archangel" because it was planned to be the home of some sick Indians. The present city dates from 1841; it became the county seat of Marin County in 1850, and was incorporated in 1874.

Feast day: historically, October 24; recently changed to September 29.

San RAMON

There are at least three saints named Raymond in the Church calendar. They are: 1) Blessed Raymond Lull, a Franciscan, who learned Arabic and preached in Tunisia and Algeria. The university in Palma, Majorca, where Fr. Serra studied and taught before coming to Mexico, had been founded by Raymond Lull in 1276. 2) St. Raymond Peñaforte (San Raymundo in Spanish), a Dominican from Catalonia, Spain (1175-1275). 3) St. Raymond Nonnatus (Unborn; so called because he was delivered from his mother's womb by Caesarian section), a Mercedarian brother (1204-1240), who ransomed Christian slaves in Africa.

The town of San Ramon in Contra Costa County was not named for any saint, but for a man named Ramon, who herded sheep in that area about 1833. It is not known for which Saint Raymond the sheep herder had been named; nor is it known precisely when, or by whom, the "San" was added to the name.

Feast days: Blessed Raymond Lull, September 5;
St. Raymond of Peñaforte, January 23 in the 19th century, January 7 today;
St. Raymond Nonnatus, August 31.

San ROQUE

St. Roch (in Italian, San Rocco) was probably born in Montpelier, southern France. Orphaned at age 20, he went on a pilgrimage to Rome, where he began a lifelong devotion to caring for the sick. Stricken with the plague himself, and left to die by the wayside, he was rescued by a dog's barking (some legends say the dog also brought food), and eventually recovered. He is depicted in art as pulling up his cloak to display a plague spot on his thigh, which some legends say was cured by the touch of an angel. He lived from 1295-1378, dying in prison at the age of 83. He became a popular saint in western Europe, and his intercession was often invoked against the plague.

The district of San Roque in the city of Santa Barbara derives its name from early ranches in that area; or it may go back to Fr. Crespí's time, when he bestowed that name on an Indian ranchería in the nearby Carpenteria area.

Feast day: August 16.

St. Isidore the Husbandman

San SIMEON

There are several saints named Simeon, at least three of them dating from New Testament times -- Simeon, the old man who held the infant Jesus in his arms and then asked for death, saying that his lifelong wish had been fulfilled; Simeon the Zealot, mentioned several times in the Gospels; and Simeon, son of Cleophas, and a cousin of Jesus. Because of language problems (Greek and Aramaic forms of the same name, etc.), we shall probably never determine the exact identities and relationships of the various people named James, Simeon, and Mary who are mentioned in the New Testament; but it is likely that this Simeon, the son of Cleophas, was martyred under the emperor Trajan about 107, at a very advanced age.

The place name of San Simeon goes back to 1819, as a rancho of Mission San Miguel. Its first post office was in 1864. The community is now completely overshadowed by the huge Hearst San Simeon State Historical Monument, a property donated by the Hearst family to the State of California, and opened to the public in 1958.

Feast day: February 18.

San TOMAS: see Appendix.

San VICENTE

This name is to be found in several localities in California, and St. Vincent Ferrer is probably the saint intended. St. Vincent (1350-1419) was a Spaniard, born of a noble family in Valencia. He had the ill-luck to be on the wrong side in the Avignon/Rome dispute as to which Pope, or series of Popes, was the legitimate successor of St. Peter. Vincent defended the Avignon line, but later in life, seeing the bad effects of the Great Western Schism, he persuaded his patron, anti-pope Benedict XIII, to resign, and so brought this schism to an end.

There is no incorporated place named San Vicente, but the boulevard of that name in the western part of Los Angeles has given rise to a large area being popularly designated the "San Vicente district."

Feast day: April 5.

San YSIDRO

There are two Spanish saints named Isidore; one, a bishop of Seville (506-636), is as famous for his great encyclopedia and his scientific treatises as for his holiness; the other, living from 1070 to 1130, was born on a farm and as a young man was a hired hand on a large estate near present-day Madrid. There he and his wife lived lives of great holiness, and after his death many miracles were reported at his grave.

The community of San Ysidro in San Diego County owes its origin to a rancho of Mission San Diego, named sometime prior to 1836 in honor of San Ysidro. This fact would seem to favor the second St. Isidore as the intended patron. St. Isidore the Husbandman, as he is sometimes called, would seem to be a more likely patron saint for a new rancho than the erudite bishop of Seville.

Feast days: St. Isidore the Husbandman, May 15 (some calendars give May 10);
St. Isidore of Seville, April 4 (some calendars give April 3).

Mission Santa Barbara

Santa ANA

St. Anne is revered throughout Christendom as the mother of the Virgin Mary; her husband was St. Joachim, and the two names are generally coupled together, and their feasts celebrated on the same day. According to legend they were from Nazareth, were married at about age twenty, but remained childless for twenty years. Both of them prayed to God, and an angel came and told Anne that, though she was then nearly forty, she would conceive. The child that was subsequently born of her was Mary of Nazareth, of whom later was born Jesus Christ.

The city of Santa Ana in Orange County is named for the large river that flows nearby. This river has the distinction of being perhaps the only natural feature named for a saint by the soldiers of the Portolá Expedition, giving evidence of the unusual devotion to St. Anne that even these rough frontier soldiers had.

Feast day of St. Anne and St. Joachim: July 26.

Santa ANITA: a diminutive form of Santa Ana.

Santa BARBARA

St. Barbara was, according to legend, the daughter of a wealthy pagan family living in some part of the Roman Empire in the 4th century. She was converted to Christianity and one time, during her father's absence on business, she ordered a third window to be built into the wall of her bathroom, in honor of the Trinity. Her father, angered at this, brought her before a magistrate, but the parent thought that she got off too easily, so he himself executed her. While returning from the hilltop where he had done the deed, he was killed by fire from heaven. St. Barbara is the patron saint of gunners, of engineers, and of architects and builders.

The Presidio of Santa Bárbara was established in 1782, but the name of the Channel and one of the offshore islands goes back to Vizcaino's visit there on December 4, 1602. The mission was established in 1786; the county was named in February 1850; and the city incorporated two months later.

Feast day: December 4.

Santa CATALINA

St. Catherine of Alexandria was, assuming she did actually exist, a contemporary of St. Barbara, and their lives were similar. Born into a wealthy family, she was converted to Christianity by a vision of Christ. Like St. Barbara she was first ordered to be tortured, by being tied to a wheel with spikes on it, which miraculously broke to pieces when it began to turn. She was then beheaded. Her body is reputed to be still at the Monastery of St. Catherine on the slopes of Mt. Sinai, which has been a place of Christian worship for over fifteen hundred years. She is the patroness of virgins as well as philosophers.

Santa Catalina Island (nowadays shortened to Catalina Island) was first so named by Vizcaino in 1602, and this name has survived, though other early explorers and map-makers have used other names at various times.

Feast day: November 25.

St. Clare

Santa CLARA

St. Clare of Assisi was a young girl of about eighteen when she was converted to a life of holiness by a sermon of St. Francis in 1212. She and her younger sister ran away from home and, under St. Francis's direction, took vows of chastity. But since St. Francis had as yet no convent for women, they lived with a group of Benedictine nuns. Later Clare founded several convents of her own, called the Poor Clares, one feature of their life being absolute poverty, not even owning their own buildings. This led to litigation, and the Pope permitted the Poor Clares to own some houses to live in, but not to inherit any income-producing property. The Poor Clares are sometimes called the Second Order of Franciscans.

Mission Santa Clara was founded in 1777, and the valley, county, and city all take their name from the mission. In southern California there is a Santa Clara River and a Santa Clarita Valley, both stemming from Fr. Crespí's visit there in 1769.

Feast day: August 11.

Santa CRUZ

This is not a saint's name, but refers to the Holy Cross on which Jesus Christ died on Calvary near Jerusalem. The name was used by several early explorers, in particular by the Portolá Expedition of 1769, for a place near San Diego; by the crew of the supply ship "San Antonio," in the same year, for one of the Channel Islands; and later on in 1769 by the Portolá men, for a creek near the present city of Santa Cruz. The Cross itself was discovered by Saint Helena (see above under her name).

Santa Cruz Mission was founded in 1791, and in 1797 the pueblo of Branciforte was established nearby, at a spot now within the city limits of Santa Cruz. There are no buildings of the mission or pueblo left today, though a replica of the mission has been built, and is visited by tourists and sometimes used for weddings.

Feast days: Finding of the True Cross, May 3;
Exaltation of the Cross, September 14.

Santa FE

Like the name Santa Cruz, this does not refer to any saint, but to the Holy Faith which inspired so many missionaries, and soldiers too, in their endeavors to bring Christianity to the pagan natives of the Southwest. The earliest, and best known, place name of Santa Fe is the pueblo of Santa Fe in New Mexico, founded about 1609. From this, indirectly, came the Santa Fe Railroad lines into California, giving rise to place names such as Santa Fe Springs in Los Angeles County.

There is no real feast day for something so intangible as the Holy Faith. Even the original name of the capital of New Mexico was given in honor of a saint -- Villa Real de San Francisco de Santa Fé, which meant "the town of St. Francis of the Holy Faith." Villa Real indicates a pueblo which had a charter from the king of Spain. So, ultimately, place names with Santa Fe in them go back to St. Francis, whose feast day is October 4.

Santa GERTRUDIS: see Appendix.

Ruins of the former *Asistencia* at Santa Margarita, San Luis Obispo County

Santa LUCIA

St. Lucy was born of a noble family in Syracuse, on the island of Sicily, during the last decades of the 3rd century. Many legends have grown up around her name. She is believed to have refused all suitors, preferring a life of virginity in Christ. Denounced as a Christian during the persecution of the emperor Diocletian, she was first condemned to a house of prostitution, but when the time came to take her there, she remained miraculously immovable. She was ordered to be burnt to death, but the flames could not touch her. Finally she was stabbed to death. She is invoked against diseases of the eye (perhaps because her name in Latin means "light.")

The range of mountains stretching from San Luis Obispo to Monterey was first called after San Martín, by Cabrillo in 1542; but Vizcaino named the range after Santa Lucía in 1602, and this name has stuck. It is said that the angle between the ocean floor and the mountain peaks of this range is the most precipitous of any maritime range in the world.

Feast day: December 13.

Santa MARGARITA

There are two St. Margaret's involved. One, St. Margaret of Cortona (Italy), is the saint of the community of Santa Margarita in San Luis Obispo County. This saint (1247-1297) was raised from the age of seven by a cruel stepmother. She eventually ran away from home and became the mistress of a wealthy playboy, bore him a child, and in general lived a life of luxury. But after nine years of this life her lover was murdered by a rival. Margaret resolved to change her way of life, did public penance, and devoted her days to helping the sick. She died in 1297, beloved by all the citizens of Cortona.

The other, St. Margaret of Antioch, is honored as a virgin and martyr, though the details of her life are more legendary than historical. She was converted to Christianity, imprisoned, tortured, and finally beheaded. Her name is honored in various rivers, mountains and canyons in San Diego and Riverside Counties.

Feast days: St. Margaret of Cortona, February 22;
St. Margaret of Antioch, July 20.

Santa MARIA

Though English-speaking Catholics frequently use the name of St. Mary for the Mother of God, as in St. Mary's College (Moraga) or St. Mary's Academy (Inglewood), the Spanish explorers preferred to use the term Nuestra Señora (Our Lady), as in Nuestra Señora la Reina de Los Angeles, the official designation of that pueblo in 1779. They also used Nuestra Señora de la Soledad (Our Lady of Solitude) when they founded a mission in the Salinas Valley in 1791 (see under Soledad, below). Another instance is the small creek and pond near Mission San Francisco de Asis, called la Laguna de Nuestra Señora de los Dolores (Our Lady of Sorrows). Today that mission in the city of San Francisco is commonly called Mission Dolores. And as early as 1602 Vizcaino named a prominent cape Punta de la Concepción, because it was discovered on December 8, feast of the Immaculate Conception of Mary.

The city of Santa Maria takes its name from an 1837 land grant of that name, and it is not known for certain whether Our Lady, or some other St. Mary, such as St. Mary Magdalene, might have been intended.

Feast day: of the dozen or more feasts of Our Lady, the most important are the Assumption, August 15, the Immaculate Conception, December 8, and the feast of Our Lady of Guadalupe, December 12.

St. Monica

Santa MONICA

St. Monica (331-387) was the mother of St. Augustine. As a teenager, Augustine gave his mother a bad time, abandoning her pious upbringing and, as he later confessed, indulging in all sorts of immorality while a student away from home. We know that he fathered an illegitimate child at about age 19, though he acknowledged the child and was faithful to his mistress for many years. But his mother never gave up hope of his conversion, prayed daily for him, and gave him love and maternal affection. Her prayers were answered; Augustine became a "born again" Christian, and later a bishop; and by his writings he became a great influence on Christianity for over a thousand years.

The mountains, city and bay of Santa Monica probably owe their name to Portolá's explorers of 1770, who passed by this way around the feast day of St. Monica, on their way to Monterey.

Feast day: May 4.

Santa NELLA

There is no St. Nella, nor is the name of this small community in Merced County a diminutive form of any other name. It owes its origin to the Rancho Centinela, part of the huge Rancho San Luis Gonzaga, belonging to the Pacheco family. "Centinela" means literally a look-out, and the ranch was probably so named because it had a hill on it which sheepherders could climb to search for stray animals. The word Centinela has become corrupted into Santa Nella, and the area is now becoming quite a community of motels and restaurants, and even has a post office, a branch of Gustine.

A feast day cannot be assigned, since there is no Saint Nella.

Santa PAULA

St. Paula was born of a noble Roman family in 347, was married to an upright young man, and was the mother of five children. Theirs was looked upon as an ideal Christian marriage. But her husband died when she was only 32, leaving her to bring up five children by herself. She later became a disciple of St. Jerome, and, accompanied by one of her daughters, she went to Bethlehem, where she founded a hospital, a monastery, and a convent. She governed the convent wisely for many years, and she is especially noted for the assistance that she gave to St. Jerome in his work of translating the Bible into the common tongue.

Santa Paula in Ventura County was once a rancho of Mission San Buenaventura (1834) and also a land grant named that same year. The city was founded in 1872 and incorporated in 1902.

Feast day: January 26.

St. Rose of Lima

Santa RITA

St. Rita (1381-1457) was married at an early age, and became the mother of two sons. Unfortunately her husband turned out to what one writer has described as "a dissolute boor," who abused her and her children for eighteen years, until he was finally murdered in a brawl. Her sons vowed to avenge his death, but their pious mother prayed that they might not commit another murder; her prayers were answered, and both of her sons later died of natural causes. The widow was then free to enter an Augustinian convent at Cascia, some 14 miles from her native Spoleto in Italy. Although not formally canonized until 1900, St. Rita was believed to be a saint from early times, and was very popular in Spain, as "the patroness of impossible cases."

The name survives in Merced County (1806), in Monterey County (1837), in Santa Barbara County (1839), and in Alameda County (also 1839).

Feast day: May 22.

Santa ROSA

St. Rose of Lima, until recently the only female saint born in the Americas, took the name Rose at her confirmation. Her full name was Isabel de Santa Maria de Flores. A beautiful girl, her parents wished her to marry, but she refused. She became a Dominican tertiary (one who lived by the Rule of St. Dominic, but stayed at home). She practiced great austerities, and went to live in a little shack on her parent's property. At the time of a great earthquake her prayers were credited with sparing the city of Lima. She died in 1586 and was canonized in 1671, the first saint, male or female, from the Americas to be canonized.

Santa Rosa in Sonoma County owes its origin, according to legend, to the baptism of an Indian girl, some time after the founding of the Sonoma Mission (1823), who was given the name Rosa after the saint. The post office dates from 1852, and the city was incorporated in 1868. There was also a land grant in Riverside County in 1845, from which today's Santa Rosa Indian Reservation takes its name.

Feast day: August 23.

Santa SUSANA

St. Susanna was of a noble Roman family, and Susanna herself was reputed to be extremely beautiful. Pope St. Caius (283) was her uncle. The emperor Diocletian wished her to marry his colleague, the co-emperor Maximian, but since the latter was little more than a peasant who had become a high-ranking army officer by brutality and intrigue, she refused. This, together with her converting to Christianity two of his favorite courtiers, so enraged Diocletian that he ordered her and her father to be beheaded. This was carried out in the year 295.

The Santa Susana pass between the San Fernando Valley of Los Angeles and the Simi Valley (Ventura County) was used by travelers for many years before the railroad came that way, building a line between Los Angeles and Ventura. The name of the pass and of the mountains occurs frequently in documents between 1804 and 1850. It is not known precisely who first gave the name, but it was probably the Franciscans of San Buenaventura Mission.

Feast day: August 11.

Santa VENETIA: see Appendix.

Mission Santa Ynez

Santa YNEZ

St. Agnes was born of a noble Roman family, and like her contemporary St. Susanna was reputed to be a beautiful young girl, who chose to dedicate herself to a life of virginity in Christ. Denounced as a Christian, she was ordered by the emperor Diocletian's magistrates to be sent to a house of prostitution, where her virginity was miraculously preserved. Unable to conquer her indomitable spirit, the emperor then ordered her to be beheaded. This was in 304. She is one of the beloved patronesses of young girls, and because of the similarity of her name to the Latin word "agnus," a lamb, she is often represented in art as holding a lamb.

Mission Santa Inés in Santa Barbara County was founded in 1804. It has the distinction of being the site of the first college in California. The College of Our Lady of Refuge opened there in 1844, but moved to another site later on, and finally closed in 1881.

Feast day: January 21.

Santa YSABEL

St. Elizabeth was the childless wife of a priest of the Temple in Jerusalem, named Zachary. They prayed to God for a child, and their prayers were answered. We know the child as St. John the Baptist. About three months before the birth of the child, Mary of Nazareth came to visit her cousin Elizabeth.

Several places in California (in San Diego and San Luis Obispo Counties) have been named for St. Elizabeth, sometimes spelled as Santa Isabel; and in Santa Clara County a peak, valley, and creek all have been named simply Isabel. There are other saints in the calendar named Elizabeth, such as St. Elizabeth of Hungary, and her grand-niece, St. Isabella of Portugal, but probably all such names stem ultimately from the biblical St. Elizabeth, mother of St. John the Baptist.

Feast day: November 15.

SANTIAGO: see Appendix.

SOLANO

San Francisco Solano (1549-1610) was an Observantine Franciscan missionary to the Indians and colonists in Argentina, Paraguay and Peru. He was noted for his sermons and for his success in making converts. He was called "Wonderworker of the New World." After many miracles were recorded, he was canonized in 1726.

Mission San Francisco Solano, usually called the Sonoma Mission, was begun as a place more healthy than Mission Dolores in San Francisco, where the damp climate was contributing to disease. Fr. Altimira proposed to close Dolores and move the sick Indians to Sonoma. The Mexican Legislature approved the plan, but the Franciscan authorities were slow to approve. When Fr. Altimira went ahead without his superior's permission, the Governor supported him and calmed down the furious Prefect of the Missions. A compromise was reached; the mission was founded, in 1823, but Mission Dolores was not closed down; and the new mission was named after San Francisco Solano, in dedication ceremonies on April 4, 1824. Today the mission is referred to as the Sonoma Mission, because of its location in that city. But the name survives in Solano County.

Feast day: July 13.

Ventura Mission (San Buenaventura)

SOLEDAD

This place in Monterey County is another shortened form of a longer title of Our Lady. According to the story recorded by Fr. Font, who said that it happened about 1769, the name arose from a misunderstanding by one of Portolá's men of an Indian's reply to his question. The reply sounded to the Spanish soldier like the word "soledad," meaning solitude, so the area acquired this name. Later, in 1791, a mission was built there, and was dedicated to Our Lady of Solitude, the latter part of the name reflecting the existing Spanish name for that area.

Besides the place in the Salinas Valley (above), there is a Soledad Canyon in Los Angeles County, and also one in San Diego County. Though given other names at other times, both of these places are now officially named Soledad, but the actual origin of the name in each case is uncertain.

TRINIDAD

The Holy Trinity (Three Persons in One God, a fundamental Christian belief) is often found in place names in the Hispanic world. In California we find the name both in Spanish and in English; in Spanish in Humbolt County, where Trinidad Bay was first entered by the Spanish ship "Santiago," captained by Bruno Heceta, and named on Trinity Sunday, 1775; and in English in Trinity County, the Trinity Alps, and other features. The latter name, according to Erwin Gudde, in his book *California Place Names*, arose from the erroneous belief that the Trinity River emptied into Trinidad Bay. It is actually a tributary of the Klamath, which runs into the ocean many miles north of Trinidad Bay.

Feast day: Trinity Sunday, the Sunday following Pentecost, which in turn is celebrated seven weeks after Easter.

VENTURA

San Buenaventura, whose name has been shortened in California to Ventura, was given the name Giovanni (John) when he was born in 1221, but St. Francis of Assisi is reported to have cured him of a childhood disease, upon which his parents changed his name (or nicknamed him) Bonaventura (Good Luck). He kept the name when he became a Franciscan himself in 1238. He became a famous theologian; in fact, in 1663 all Spanish Franciscan teachers were required from that time on to teach no other doctrine but that of St. Bonaventure, even though it included the anti-Copernican doctrine that the earth, not the sun, was the center of the solar system. Fr. Serra, in the 18th century, therefore had to teach this to his Mallorcan university students, before he became a missionary in California.

The mission named for him in Ventura was founded on Easter Sunday, 1782, and it remains a parish church and tourist attraction to this day.

Feast day: July 15.

APPENDIX

Asunción [San Luis Obispo County]: An early land grant, and later a railroad station. The name refers to the Assumption of Our Lady. Feast day: August 15

Carmel [Monterey County]: The nearby river was named by Vizcaino in 1603, to honor the Carmelite chaplains of his expedition. The Carmelite Order claims the prophet Elias as one of its founders. The connection between Elias and Mt. Carmel may be read in the Bible, in I(III) Kings:18.

Madonna [Santa Clara County]: Mount Madonna was named by an early immigrant. It is the Italian version of Nuestra Señora, and means literally My Lady. (The Madonna Inn south of San Luis Obispo is named by, and for, a local contractor of that name).

Natividad Creek [Monterey County]: Named in 1776, a few days before the feast of the Annunciation, not for the actual Nativity of Christ, but for the Announcement of this event nine months earlier. See under San Gabriel in the text.

Refugio [Santa Barbara County]: The beach, pass, and rancho are named for Nuestra Señora del Refugio (Our Lady of Refuge), as are other land grants in other counties.

San Agustin Creek [Santa Cruz County]: Named for St. Augustine of Hippo. See under Santa Monica, above. Feast day: August 28.

San Benancio Gulch [Monterey County]: Named for St. Venantius Fortunatus, a 6th century bishop, who also wrote many poems and hymns. Feast day: December 14.

San Bernarbé [Monterey County]: A land grant, named for St. Barnabas, one of the twelve Apostles. Feast day: June 11.

San Cajetano Mountain [Ventura County]: Named for St. Cajetan, a 16th century Italian church reformer. He is the originator of pawn shops. Feast day: August 7.

San Carpoforo Creek [Monterey County]: Named for St. Carpophorus, martyred about 306. Feast day: November 8.

San (or Santo) Domingo: Several natural features in California are named for St. Dominic (1170-1271), famous preacher, and founder of the Dominican friars. Feast day: August 8.

San Elijo Lagoon [San Diego County]: Named for St. Alexis, a 5th century "man of God." The name is also spelled Alejo in Spanish. Feast day: July 17.

San Emigdio [Kern County]: A land grant and rancho, named for St. Emygdius, an early Christian martyr. He is invoked as a patron against earthquakes. Feast day: August 9.

San Felipe: Several creeks and valleys, in various counties, are named for St. Philip, one of the twelve Apostles. Feast day: May 3.

San Gorgonio Mountain [San Bernardino County]: Named for one of two saints of this name, both early martyrs. The more probable one died in 303. Feast day: March 12.

San Julian [Santa Barbara County]: A land grant, named for a legendary St. Julian, who unknowingly murdered his own parents. He did penance for this crime and was forgiven when he took a leper into his home and cared for him. Feast day: February 12.

San Luis Dam [Merced County]: Indirectly named for St. Aloysius Gonzaga, a 16th century Italian Jesuit, who died at the early age of 23. Feast day: June 21.

San Marin [Marin County]: A real estate development west of Novato. There is no Saint Marin, and the name does not appear to be a variant of San Marino. For a discussion of the various possible origins of the name of Marin County, see Erwin G. Gudde, *California Place Names*, 3rd. ed., pp. 192-193.

San Tomás Creek [Santa Clara County]: Named for the great Scholastic philosopher and theologian, St. Thomas Aquinas (1225-1274). Feast day: January 28.

Santa Gertrudis: A name given to several early land grants in Southern California. Probably St. Gertrude of Saxony (1256-1302) is the saint intended. Feast day: November 16.

Santa Venetia [Marin County]: A residential community near San Rafael, started in 1914. Real estate developers coined the name. There is no Saint Venetia.

Santiago Creek [Orange County]: Named in 1769 for St. James, one of the twelve Apostles. He is reputed to have preached in Spain, but he died in Palestine. He is the patron saint of Spain, and pilgrims still visit his shrine at Compostela. Feast day: July 25.

Visitación [San Francisco County]: A valley (now a district of south-eastern San Francisco), named in honor of the visit paid by Our Lady to St. Elizabeth. See under Santa Ysabel in the text. Feast day: July 2.

ABOUT THE AUTHOR

Raymund F. Wood was born in England, but came to California in his high school years. He obtained a Ph.D. in History from UCLA, and has since published many books and articles on California history, including several on the missions and missionaries. His principal hobbies are book collecting, maps, and photography.

ABOUT THE ILLUSTRATOR

Anthony Quartuccio, a long-time resident of San Jose, has been winning awards for his art work ever since his junior high school days. He studied at the Jean Turner Art School in San Francisco, and has worked as artist-construction specialist for Ames Research Laboratory (NASA) at Moffet Field. His earlier publications have included *Rambling Through Baja California with Pen and Brush*, and *Santa Clara Valley, California; an Artist's View, Today and Yesterday*.